MAY 2017

SandCastle

Word Families Set 8

-ain as in train

Carey Molter

Consulting Editor Monica Marx, M.A./Reading Specialist

ABDO
Publishing Company

Published by SandCastle™, an imprint of ABDO Publishing Company, 4940 Viking Drive, Edina, Minnesota 55435.

Printed in the United States.

Credits
Edited by: Pam Price
Curriculum Coordinator: Nancy Tuminelly
Cover and Interior Design and Production: Mighty Media
Photo Credits: Hemera, Donna Day/ImageState, PhotoDisc

Library of Congress Cataloging-in-Publication Data

Molter, Carey, 1973-
    -Ain as in train / Carey Molter.
       p. cm. -- (Word families. Set VIII)
    Summary: Introduces, in brief text and illustrations, the use of the letter combination "ain" in such words as "train," "sprain," "chain," and "brain."
    ISBN 1-59197-272-8
    1. Readers (Primary) [1. Vocabulary. 2. Reading.] I. Title.

PE1119 .M58 2003
428.1--dc21   2002038212

SandCastle™ books are created by a professional team of educators, reading specialists, and content developers around five essential components that include phonemic awareness, phonics, vocabulary, text comprehension, and fluency. All books are written, reviewed, and leveled for guided reading, early intervention reading, and Accelerated Reader® programs and designed for use in shared, guided, and independent reading and writing activities to support a balanced approach to literacy instruction.

Let Us Know

After reading the book, SandCastle would like you to tell us your stories about reading. What is your favorite page? Was there something hard that you needed help with? Share the ups and downs of learning to read. We want to hear from you! To get posted on the ABDO Publishing Company Web site, send us e-mail at:

sandcastle@abdopub.com

SandCastle Level: Transitional

-ain Words

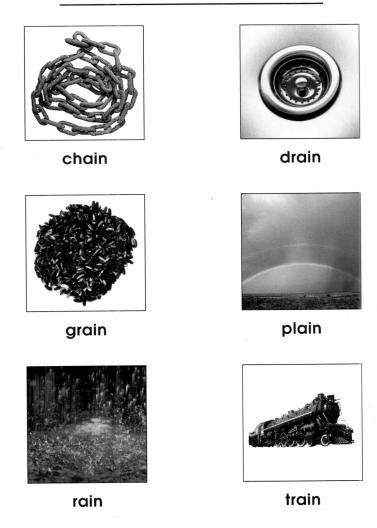

chain

drain

grain

plain

rain

train

Jane made a flower chain.

The drain is in the
bottom of the sink.

Rice is a grain.

A plain is large and flat.

Rain falls from the sky.

Clark fixes the train.

Cain the Train in Spain

In Spain there was a train.

The train's name was Cain.

Cain carried grain
through Spain.

Sometimes it would rain.

The rain was mainly
on the plain.

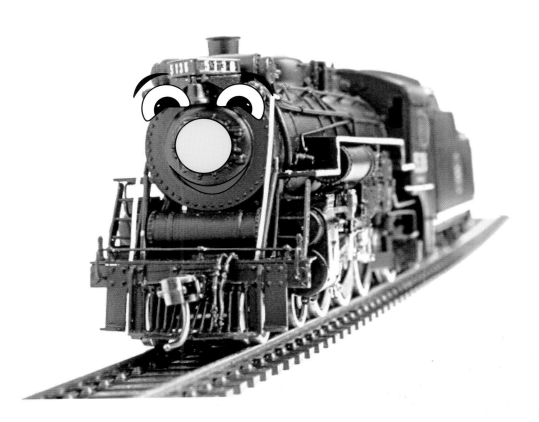

Cain was an old train.

Going over the plain
was a strain for Cain.

What a pain!

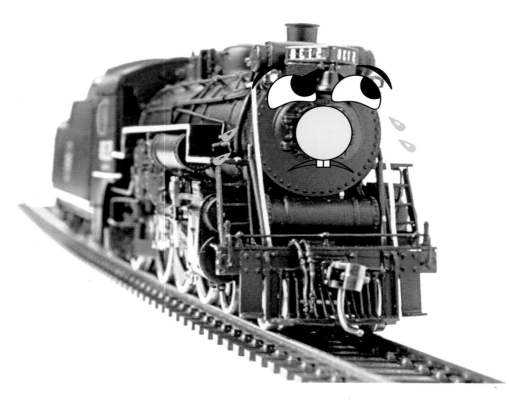

Cain tried not to
complain.

"The plain is a strain,"
he would explain.

His friend pulled Cain
with a chain.

What a great
friend to gain
on the plain
in Spain!

The -ain Word Family

brain	pain
chain	plain
drain	slain
gain	sprain
grain	strain
lain	train
main	vain

Glossary

Some of the words in this list may have more
than one meaning. The meaning listed here
reflects the way the word is used in the book.

chain   a series of connected links

drain   a pipe that waste water
goes through

grain   the seed of cereal plants,
like rice and wheat

plain   a large, flat area of land
that is usually treeless

strain   extreme effort, exertion, or
work

About SandCastle™

A professional team of educators, reading specialists, and content developers created the SandCastle™ series to support young readers as they develop reading skills and strategies and increase their general knowledge. The SandCastle™ series has four levels that correspond to early literacy development in young children. The levels are provided to help teachers and parents select the appropriate books for young readers.

Emerging Readers
(no flags)

Beginning Readers
(1 flag)

Transitional Readers
(2 flags)

Fluent Readers
(3 flags)

These levels are meant only as a guide. All levels are subject to change.

To see a complete list of SandCastle™ books and other nonfiction titles from ABDO Publishing Company, visit www.abdopub.com or contact us at:

4940 Viking Drive, Edina, Minnesota 55435 • 1-800-800-1312 • fax: 1-952-831-1632